SOIL

BY SALLY M. WALKER

LERNER PUBLICATIONS COMPANY • MINNEAPOLIS

The photographs in this book are used with the permission of: PhotoDisc Royalty Free by Getty Images, pp. 1, 1(title type), 4, 6 (background), 9, 10 (background), 24 (background), 28 (background), 32, 37, 38 (both), 40, 44–45 (background), 46–47 (background); © Yoshio Tomii/SuperStock, p. 5; © Dana Richter/Visuals Unlimited, p. 6; © Mark A. Schneider/Visuals Unlimited, p. 7; © Royalty-Free/CORBIS, pp. 8, 25; © Dr. Marli Miller/Visuals Unlimited, pp. 10, 15, 23; © John R. Kreul/Independent Picture Service, p. 11; © Robert & Jean Pollock/ Visuals Unlimited, p. 12; courtesy of Captain Budd Christman/National Oceanic and Atmospheric Administration Central Library Photo Collection, p. 13; © Adam Jones/Visuals Unlimited, p. 14; USDA Photo, p. 16; © Dr. Dennis Kunkel/Visuals Unlimited, pp. 17, 30; © R. F. Ashley/Visuals Unlimited, p. 18; © Todd Strand/Independent Picture Service, pp. 19, 21 (both); U.S. Geological Survey Photo Library, pp. 20, 24; © Gilbert Twiest/Visuals Unlimited, p. 22; © Dr. G. Prance/Visuals Unlimited, p. 26; © John Sohlden/Visuals Unlimited, p. 28; © Todd Strand/Independent Picture Service, with permission from Munsell/Division of GretagMacbeth, LLC., p. 29; © age fotostock/SuperStock, pp. 33, 41; © Wally Eberhart/Visuals Unlimited, pp. 34, 35, 48 (top); © Natalia Brand/SuperStock, p. 36; © Mark Gibson/Visuals Unlimited, p. 39; © Pegasus/Visuals Unlimited, p. 43; © Dr. John D. Cunningham/Visuals Unlimited, p. 46; © Bill Banaszewski/Visuals Unlimited, p. 47; © Tom Edwards/Visuals Unlimited, p. 48 (bottom).

Front Cover: © Royalty-Free/CORBIS
Front Cover Title Type: PhotoDisc Royalty Free by Getty Images
Back Cover: © Reuters/CORBIS
Illustrations on pp. 27, 31, 42 by Laura Westlund, copyright © by Independent Picture Service.

Copyright © 2007 by Sally M. Walker

Lerner Publications Company
A division of Lerner Publishing Group
241 First Avenue North
Minneapolis, MN 55401 U.S.A.

Website address: www.lernerbooks.com

Library of Congress Cataloging-in-Publication Data

Walker, Sally M.
  Soil / by Sally M. Walker.
    p.   cm. — (Early bird Earth science)
  Includes index.
  ISBN-13: 978-0-8225-5948-1 (lib. bdg. : alk. paper)
  ISBN-10: 0-8225-5948-X (lib. bdg. : alk. paper)
  1. Soils—Juvenile literature. 2. Soil ecology—Juvenile literature. I. Title. II. Series.
  S591.3.W35 2007
  631.4—dc22
                                                              2005032222

Manufactured in the United States of America
1 2 3 4 5 6 – JR – 12 11 10 09 08 07

CONTENTS

BE A WORD DETECTIVE

Can you find these words as you read about soil? Be a
detective and try to figure out what they mean. You can
turn to the glossary on page 46 for help.

bacteria	horizon	nutrients
bedrock	humus	particles
clay	loam	sand
conserve	minerals	silt
glaciers	natural resource	textures

This field has good soil. A farmer will grow plants in the soil. What are some other places where soil can be found?

CHAPTER 1
WHAT IS SOIL?

Did you ever make mud pies when you were little? If you did, soil was one of the ingredients you used. You may have called it dirt instead of soil.

Trees' roots grow deep into the soil.

Soil is in lots of places. You can find soil under the grass. It surrounds tree and flower roots. It lies beneath sidewalks and streets. If you could lift your house, you would probably find soil under it too!

A scoop of soil contains many things. Soil has rocks in it. Plants and bits of leaves are in soil. Many creatures live in soil too.

You can be a soil detective. See what you can find in the soil near your home. You will need a shovel. Ask an adult where you may dig. Use your shovel to dig out several handfuls of soil. Look closely at your soil. What can you find in it?

If you look closely at soil, you may find worms, insects, or other animals living in it.

These plants need soil to grow.

Soil is a natural resource (REE-sors). Natural resources are materials found on Earth that help living things. They are made by nature, not people. Soil helps plants and animals grow. They cannot live without it. But where does soil come from?

Hard rocks can break into small pieces. How can water break rocks?

CHAPTER 2

HOW SOIL FORMS

Soil is made up of different kinds of materials. One of these materials is bits of rock. Rocks are broken pieces of bedrock. Bedrock is the layer of solid rock that covers the outside of Earth.

10

As water rushes down this hill, it breaks off bits of rock.

Rocks are hard. But they can be broken into tiny bits. Tiny bits are called particles (PART-ih-kuhlz). Water, ice, and wind are strong enough to break rocks.

Rushing water in rivers makes rocks roll and tumble. The rocks break into smaller pieces. Tiny particles of rock break loose.

Rainwater seeps into cracks in rocks. If it gets cold enough, the water freezes. It becomes ice. Ice takes up more space than water. So the ice pushes against the rock. It makes the cracks bigger. Pieces of rock break off.

Ice split this huge rock in half.

This glacier is flowing downhill. As it moves, it carries rocks with it.

Glaciers (GLAY-sherz) are giant, moving slabs of ice. Glaciers are very heavy. Their weight slowly grinds big rocks into small pieces.

Wind blows sand grains against big rocks. The sand grains scrub off particles of rock.

Rocks are made of minerals (MIHN-ur-uhlz). A mineral is a hard substance made in nature. Minerals are not alive, like plants or animals. The minerals in a rock become part of the soil when the rock breaks apart.

Grains of sand are tiny. But if the wind blows them hard enough, they can break off bits of rock.

The flat sides on these rocks were made by blowing sand.

Minerals are an important part of soil. They add nutrients (NOO-tree-uhnts) to soil. Nutrients are substances that help living things grow. Soil contains nutrients that plants and animals need to stay healthy.

Bacteria are turning these dead leaves into humus.

Humus (HYOO-muhs) is the second material that is in soil. Humus is dark brown or black. It is made of bits of dead plants and animals.

Humus is made by bacteria (bak-TEER-ee-uh). Bacteria are tiny living things. They are so tiny that they can be seen only with a microscope. Microscopes are tools that make small things look big.

Bacteria eat dead plants and animals. They break the plants and animals into tiny pieces. The pieces become humus. Humus contains nutrients that had been inside the plants and animals. The nutrients can become part of the soil.

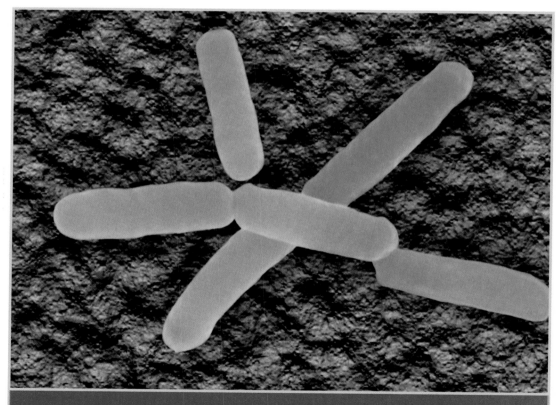

There are many kinds of bacteria. They live nearly everywhere on Earth. This picture shows one kind of bacteria that lives in soil.

Air is the third material in soil. Soil is full of air spaces. Some air spaces are large. You can easily see them. You can see the tunnels that earthworms dig in soil. An earthworm's hole is filled with air. Soil also has tiny air spaces. The tiny spaces are between bits of minerals and humus. Most of these spaces are too small for you to see. But they are there.

As earthworms move through the soil, they make tunnels.

Air fills the spaces between these rocks.

Put a handful of marbles or small rocks in a jar. Can you see spaces between the marbles or rocks? Air fills these spaces. Now imagine that you can shrink the marbles or rocks. Imagine making them as tiny as the smallest particles in soil. The air spaces would still be there. They would just be much smaller.

Water is the fourth material found in soil. Water can move around in soil. It trickles through the soil's air spaces. The moving water picks up nutrients from the soil. The water carries the nutrients into the roots of plants.

Water has filled the air spaces in this soil.

When you pour water onto the soil, the water flows down between the rocks. The water carries bits of soil with it.

Water also carries tiny particles of soil into the big air spaces. Put a handful of soil on top of the marbles or rocks in your jar. Pour in a small glass of water. Where does the water go? What happens to the particles of soil?

Soil forms on flat land. It forms alongside rivers. It forms on forest floors and on low hills. Soil forms as humus and rock particles begin to pile up. It can take hundreds of years for 1 inch of soil to form.

Deep soil has formed on this flat land.

Soil can't form on the steep sides of this mountain.

Soil cannot form in some places. Soil cannot form on steep mountains. That's because soil-making materials slide down the mountain. Soil cannot form in very windy places or places where water flows quickly. In these places, soil-making materials can't pile up. They do not have enough time to become soil.

23

We usually see only the top of the soil. What is this soil mostly made of?

CHAPTER 3
LAYERS OF SOIL

If you dig deep down into the ground, you may notice different colors of soil. These are different layers of soil. A layer is a single thickness of soil. A blanket lying on your bed is a layer. A cake may have several layers. Soil has layers too.

This soil is made mostly of humus. It is full of nutrients that growing plants need.

A soil layer is called a horizon (huh-RYE-zuhn). The horizon that is closest to the surface is called the A horizon. This layer is made mostly of humus. The A horizon has many nutrients. It helps plants grow.

Under the A horizon is the B horizon. The B horizon has less humus. It has more sand and small rocks.

You can see different layers in this soil.

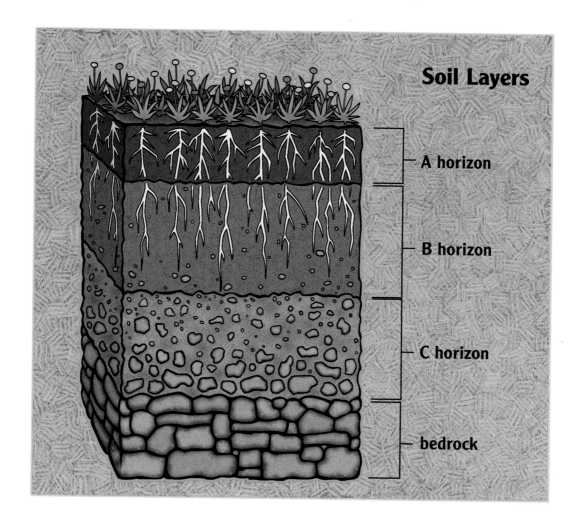

A horizon

B horizon

C horizon

bedrock

The C horizon is the deepest soil layer. It is just above the bedrock. The soil in the C horizon has lots of big, chunky rocks. The A and B horizons cover the C horizon. They protect the C horizon from water, ice, and wind.

Most soils are brownish. But some are other colors, such as red. What gives soil its color?

CHAPTER 4
WHAT SOIL LOOKS LIKE

Soil can be made of many different kinds of minerals. Different minerals can be different colors. The minerals and humus in soil help give the soil its color. Many soils are a shade of brown. But some are yellow. Some are even bright orange red.

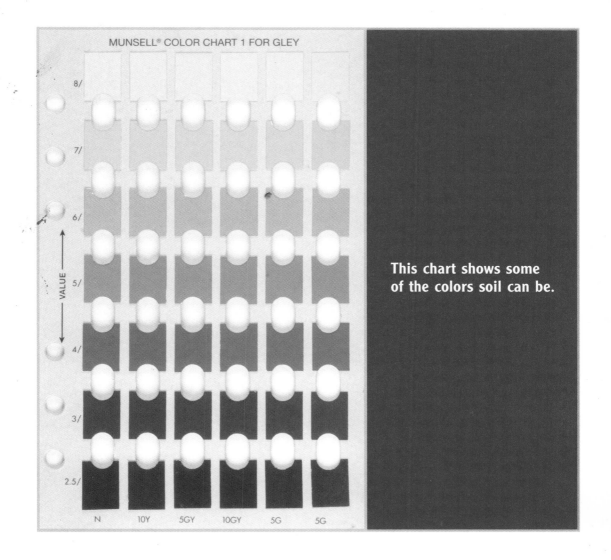

8/

7/

6/

VALUE

5/

4/

3/

2.5/

N　　10Y　　5GY　　10GY　　5G　　5G

**This chart shows some
of the colors soil can be.**

Soil also has different textures (TEKS-chuhrz). Texture is how rough or smooth something is. The texture of soil depends on the size of the soil's particles.

Some of these sand grains have sharp edges. Others are smoother.

The largest mineral particles in soil are called sand. You can see the mineral particles in sandy soil. Sand particles feel rough when you rub them between your fingers. Some sand-sized particles have sharp, jagged edges. Others are mostly round.

Another kind of particle in soil is called silt. Silt particles are much smaller than sand particles. It's hard to see silt particles. If you rub silt between your fingers, it feels smooth. Silt-sized particles are shaped like sand particles.

Clay particles are the smallest particles in soil. They are too small to see without a microscope. Clay particles are flat.

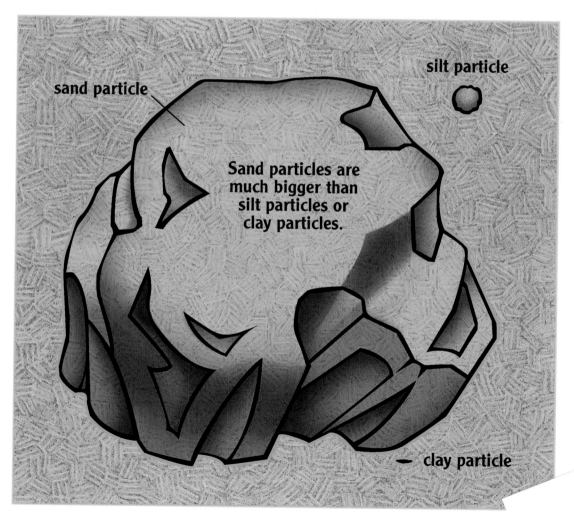

silt particle

sand particle

Sand particles are much bigger than silt particles or clay particles.

clay particle

Water drains quickly through sand. That's why you won't see puddles in wet sand at the beach.

Sand particles have big air spaces between them. Water drains quickly through the spaces. So puddles rarely form in sandy soil. Silt particles have smaller spaces between them. Water takes longer to drain through small spaces. Flat clay particles get squeezed together. The spaces between clay particles are tiny. Water has a hard time trickling through tiny air spaces. Clay particles also soak up water. So it takes a long time for water to drain through soil that has a lot of clay.

Water drains slowly through clay particles. When it rains, puddles often form in soil that has many clay particles.

Soil with equal amounts of sand, silt, and clay particles is called loam (LOHM). Loam is very good for growing plants. It holds just the right amount of water for growing roots.

This soil is loam. Most plants grow well in loam.

This picture shows **sandy soil** (left), **loam** (middle), **and clay soil** (right).

Soil that has mostly sand-sized particles is called sandy loam. Water drains quickly through sandy loam.

Soil with mostly clay-sized particles is called clay loam. Water drains slowly through clay loam. Rain often forms puddles in clay loam.

What kind of texture does your soil have? Rub the soil between your fingers. Does it feel rough, smooth, or in-between?

Different soils have different textures.

When wet clay loam dries out, it breaks into hard chunks.

Put some soil in your palm. Add a small amount of water to your soil. Add only enough to make the soil moist. If it seems too wet, add a little more soil. Mix the soil and water together with your fingers. See if you can mold the soil into a flat circle. If you can, your soil has a lot of clay. If the circle crumbles, the soil contains more sand and silt than clay.

We need soil so trees and other plants can grow. What happens when people spray chemicals outside?

CHAPTER 5

TAKING CARE OF SOIL

Soil is a very important natural resource. It takes a long time for soil to form. So we must take good care of Earth's soil.

Farmers often spray chemicals on their fields.

People often use chemicals (KEHM-ih-kuhlz) to kill harmful bugs or weeds. Some of these chemicals may stay in the soil. The chemicals can hurt animals, people, and other plants. So people must be careful not to use too much of these chemicals.

This place was once a forest. People cut down most of the trees. Rain has washed away a lot of the soil.

Tree roots help hold soil in place. Cutting down too many trees leaves the soil unprotected. Then water and wind can sweep the soil away.

Farmers plant crops in soil. A crop is a kind of plant, such as corn or wheat. A farmer can damage soil by planting the same crop in the same field year after year. The crop uses up the soil's nutrients. After a while, plants can no longer grow in that field. Wise farmers conserve soil. Conserving soil means using it wisely. Growing different crops every few years keeps a field's soil healthy. Then the field can be used for a longer time.

Different kinds of crops are growing on this farm.

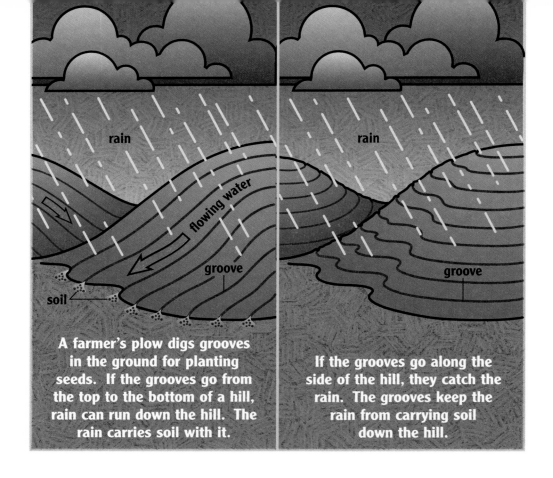

A farmer's plow digs grooves in the ground for planting seeds. If the grooves go from the top to the bottom of a hill, rain can run down the hill. The rain carries soil with it.

If the grooves go along the side of the hill, they catch the rain. The grooves keep the rain from carrying soil down the hill.

Farmers also conserve soil by plowing their fields the right way. Plowing is breaking up the soil. Plowing makes grooves in the soil so crops can be planted in rows. If the grooves go straight down a hill, rain can easily wash soil away. Instead, the farmer can make grooves that circle around the hill. Then the grooves make ridges of soil. The ridges stop rain from flowing down the hill. The soil stays in place.

The next time you go outside, look at the soil around you. Notice its color. See what kinds of plants are growing in it. Feel its texture.

Watch how people take care of the soil. Try to think of ways that you can care for the soil around your house. Plants, animals, and people will always need healthy soil!

Taking care of the soil is important.

LEARN MORE ABOUT
SOIL

BOOKS

Bial, Raymond. *A Handful of Dirt.* New York: Walker, 2000.

Ditchfield, Christin. *Soil.* New York: Children's Press, 2002.

Lavies, Bianca. *Compost Critters.* New York: Dutton Children's Books, 1993.

Silverstein, Alvin, and Virginia Silverstein. *Life in a Bucket of Soil.* Mineola, NY: Dover Publications, 2000.

Stewart, Melissa. *Soil.* Chicago: Heinemann Library, 2002.

WEBSITES

The Dirt on Soil
http://school.discovery.com/schooladventures/soil/
Learn about the layers of soil and some of the creatures that live there, then go on an underground adventure.

Kids and Conservation
http://www.clarkswcd.org/Kids/KidsHome.htm
Learn how people can conserve soil, water, and wildlife.

Mineral Matters
http://www.sdnhm.org/kids/minerals/
This website has information about minerals, instructions for growing your own crystals, puzzles, and more.

Soil Layers
http://www.enchantedlearning.com/geology/soil/
This Web page has information about all of the soil's layers.

GLOSSARY

bacteria: tiny living things that can be seen only with a microscope

bedrock: the layer of solid rock that covers the outside of Earth

clay: the smallest mineral particles in soil

conserve: to keep something from being lost or wasted

glaciers (GLAY-sherz): giant, moving slabs of ice. Glaciers form in places that are cold all year long.

horizon (huh-RYE-zuhn): a layer of soil

humus (HYOO-muhs): a dark brown or black substance that is a part of soil. Humus is made of bits of dead plants and animals.

loam (LOHM): soil that has equal amounts of sand, silt, and clay particles. Loam is very good for growing plants.

minerals (MIHN-ur-uhlz): hard substances that are made in nature. Minerals are not alive, like plants or animals.

natural resource (REE-sors): a material found on Earth that helps living things. It is made by nature, not people.

nutrients (NOO-tree-uhnts): substances that help living things grow

particles (PART-ih-kuhlz): tiny bits

sand: the largest mineral particles in soil

silt: medium-sized mineral particles in soil. Silt particles are smaller than sand particles but larger than clay particles.

textures (TEKS-chuhrz): the roughness or smoothness of different objects

INDEX

Pages listed in **bold** type refer to photographs.